CENTER FOR THE STUDY OF
THE PASSION OF CHRIST AND THE HOLY SHROUD

GUIDE
to the Photographic Exhibit of the
HOLY SHROUD

By Msgr. GIULIO RICCI, President

MILWAUKEE, WISCONSIN

Originally published in Italian and Spanish
by the Centro Romano di Sindonologia, Rome, Italy

CONTENTS

I dedicate this guide to visitors to the photographic exhibit on the Holy Shroud. May it be a reminder of an encounter, rich in hope and in the forgiveness of sins, with this document of Christ's sufferings. The Holy Shroud reveals to us the love of God the Father, written with the Blood shed by His Son in His *divinely blessed Passion and Death* (St. Ignatius of Antioch, martyr).

Msgr. Giulio Ricci

Easter, 1982.

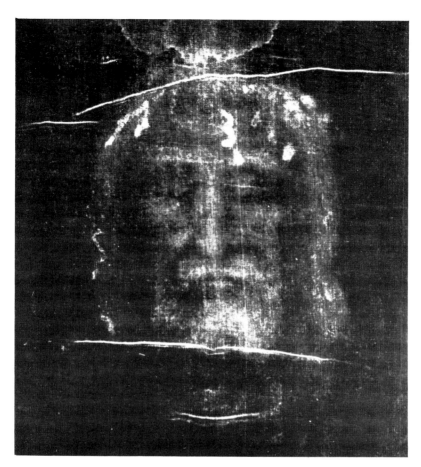

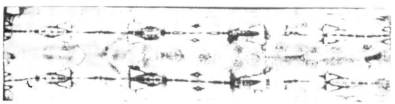

He was despised and rejected by men
   A man of sorrows, and acquainted with grief,
And as one from whom men hide their faces,
   He was despised, and we esteemed him not.

Isaiah 53

EVANGELIZATION AND THE HOLY SHROUD

EVANGELIZATION AND THE HOLY SHROUD:

PASTORAL IMPACT OF THE MESSAGE OF THE HOLY SHROUD

God's most challenging message to mankind is a message of love: man's eternal salvation through the redemptive work of the Son of God, incarnate, dead and risen. The credibility of this message, entrusted orally to the prophets and, in the fulness of time, to the Messiah Himself, by Him to the Apostles and through them to the Church, is based on the very authority of God Who revealed it.

The oral message was written down by the authors of the Old and New Testaments and by the Magisterium, which ensures it is authentically transmitted and taught.

I consider it to be quite legitimate to place the Holy Shroud on a par with this tradition written in pen and ink. The Shroud is truly a page of palæography in a unique, unrepeatable edition. Here we read God's love, written in letters of blood.

A document is characterized by the message it proffers: now if the Shroud is genuine, its message merits the same respect with which Jesus unrolled the scroll of Isaiah[1] in the synagogue in Nazareth that Sabbath day, applying the text to His messianic work. We could interpret this document in a genuine prophetic sense, reading, not on a parchment scroll but on a long linen sheet, that very same message of salvation. Our text is not written by Isaiah nor his scribe, but is rather an archetype, imprinted by remarkable contact with His humanity. It is expressed

---

[1] Cf. *Lk* 4:17-21

not in ink but in His blood.

This is why scientific research concerning its authenticity is of such enormous importance. Once it can be shown to be genuine, the message it contains can equally be demonstrated to be reliable.

At present, we have two tendencies. On the one hand, we note ever more clearly the perfect accord of our 'reading' of the Shroud with the Gospel narrative of Jesus' passion, death and resurrection. On the other hand, we are being asked whether this fact authorizes us to go beyond the anthropological view which restricts identification of the Man of the Shroud to one of any number of crucified men in the course of history, and later assimilated, by some inexplicable fortuitous coincidence, to the case of 'Jesus of Nazareth'. If, however, the Man of the Shroud can be identified with Him, we should find ourselves viewing the plan of salvation ' from the inside ', clearly revealing to us in a direct, because visual manner, both the scientific aspect (for those who have faith in the Man-God Redeemer) and also the merely historical side — albeit existential and ever-valid — even for those who do not share our faith.

It is from this very identification that the afore-mentioned assimilation would derive its importance, as emphasized by Christ Himself and by the Magisterium of the Church, when we are presented with Him in our suffering brother — He, the 'firstborn of many brothers',[2] assimilated to us in all things but sin, and assimilating us all to Him inasmuch as our earthly life associates us with His redemptive work, by virtue of His passion and death.

Thus in either case it would be legitimate to appeal to the Shroud (presuming the identification of the Man of the Shroud with Jesus) as an effective tool of evangelization for those far off, and an arresting means of re-evangelization for a dechristianized world where the majority has never known a serious catechumenate.

It will also prove an effective challenge at all levels of spirituality, where it can enrich the measure of charitable love required of man by God — love without measure — realized and presented as a perfect, effective example in His free giving of the innocent Son of God, obedient even to death on the cross.

[2] Cf *Col* 1:15-18; *Rom* 8:28; *Hebr* 1:6.

THE CONTENT OF THE MESSAGE

What is this evangelization of which we speak? At the beginnings of the Christian community, the Christian message was concentrated in the basic, kerygmatic proclamation. Only later was this expressed by an ordered and complete exposition, proper to catechesis, as started by the apologists, and profounder, theological systems (St. Irenæus). This proclamation gave major emphasis to the 'facts', the 'events', by means of which Christ announced and realized our salvation, for St. Luke gives us to understand that Jesus first began to do and then to teach.[3]

This was the secret which made the primitive message such a ferment, a potentially explosive nucleus, capable itself of suggesting by its mere affirmation, proclaimed and confirmed by miracles and wonders on the part of its herald (St. Peter),[4] along with the witnesses of the same paschal events, that Christ was the Lord, the Living One, for He was risen from the dead: an historical motif which ended in soteriology.

Let me quote for everyone the first discourse of St. Peter: «Jesus of Nazareth, a man attested to you by God with mighty works and wonders... this Jesus, delivered up according to the definite plan and foreknowledge of God, you crucified and killed by the hands of lawless men. But God raised him up... and of that we all are witnesses».[5]

In the First Letter of St. Peter we read: « If you do suffer for righteousness' sake, you will be blessed. ... for Christ also died for sins once for all, the righteous for the unrighteous, that he might bring us to God, being put to death in the flesh but made alive in the Spirit... ».[6]

In this basic, primitive proclamation we hear resounding the authority of Christ, the living Gospel of the Father, and the first and greatest evangelizer.[7] He achieved the greatest expression of evangelization in the final events of His life: His divine passion, His death and His glorious resurrection.[8] These 'evangelizing facts', are supremely convincing and effective, being the sublime revelation of God's love for men and the

---

[3] Cf. *Acts* 1:1.
[4] Cf. *Acts* 2:14.
[5] *Acts* 2:22-24, 32.
[6] *1 Pt* 3:14, 18.
[7] Paul VI, Apostolic Exhortation *Evangelii Nuntiandi,* paras. 6, 7, 8ff.
[8] Q.v. St. Ignatius of Antioch, *Ad Smyrn.,* ch. 1.

fulfilment of our hope.

To return to the assumption we have made: we note an ever closer connection between the message handed down by Christ and the message contained in the archæological 'document' we are considering — « ... he suffered under Pontius Pilate, died and was buried, and the third day he rose again according to the Scriptures... ».

Does the Shroud truly contain this central message of our faith, continuously handed down by the Church? And, if it contains it, what degree of agreement does it show with the Gospels, the primary source for the faith handed down?

The reply to these two complementary questions will provide the full justification for employing (or else rejecting) the 'document' in question as an instrument of evangelization, which, by reason of this very same agreement, will receive an extra feature of importance from various scientific tests, including those at present in course and to be completed, namely: the agreement of the imprint on the Shroud with the Gospels of the Passion. Without this confirmation, revealed by the presence of this remarkable imprint, all the other tests would be more or less futile: we should, in fact, have no criteria at our disposal to reach an adequate solution to the problem of the authenticity of this sheet, other than the fragmentary evidence concerning its transmission. This will explain why the interpretation of this 'document' requires the complete collaboration of all those engaged in research on it.

I would therefore like to state that it is from the language of various scientific research (a language which corresponds fully with human psychology) that we shall see emerging in ever greater clarity this unmistakeable harmony with the Gospel.

THE SHROUD AND THE GOSPELS

The archæological information obtained from our 'reading' of the Shroud concerning the application of penal procedure corresponds with Jesus' times. These data are connected with the person of Pontius Pilate, and reveal how he kept his word, as far as regards the scourging, and how he broke it, as far as regards his solemn promise of liberation.[9] All

---

[9] Cf. *Lk* 23:16.

this demonstrates unpardonable inconsistency in the trial under discussion.

The brutal treatment inflicted on this crucified Man, causing His rapid decease, will be shown from an analysis of the angles and the most scientifically advanced photographic techniques. The new Shroud,[10] of a rare weave, contrasts with the old rags ordinarily used for executed men. This will bring home to us the daring of Joseph of Arimathæa, who kept his discipleship hidden for fear of the Jews.[11] He managed to save his Master from the ignominious burial of the common grave, obtaining from the Roman judge permission for an honourable burial. All this refers to the permission granted by Pilate in accordance with the Roman legislative norm (the tenth of the Twelve Tablets). The Roman norm was more benevolent than the Jewish one, for it permitted, by way of an exception, a Jew who had died on the cross to be buried in the unused tomb of a rich man. The burial was hurried and incomplete, owing to the imminence of the Sabbath rest. Thus it was not possible to perform the ritual washings of the body. These ablutions could also have been performed after the Sabbath.

These are the facts which form the *background* of the account of Christ's Passion. But even more surprising is the confirmation of the analytical examination of the signs imprinted on the Shroud itself.

Let us now read, with the Gospel in our hand, the account of the death and resurrection of the Man of the Shroud, written in letters of blood.

The Scourging. The details which constitute exceptions to the general rule are those pieces of information which are usually considered normal in the Gospel account, but which, when viewed from an archæological or exegetical stance, appear as real exceptions, either owing to the fact itself, or else the manner in which it occurred. The fact of the scourging is quite clear: it was supposed to be a punishment complete in itself, prior to liberation; but the manner in which it was carried out in this case is of primary interest. According to the Gospel, Jesus was to be flogged by way of an *example* — the Greek text speaks of a scourging as a *lesson* — but the Man's life was to be spared: these

---

[10] *Mt* 27:59.
[11] *Jn* 19:38.

were the explicit orders of the judge, who intended freeing Him,[12] having recognized that He was innocent.

The *exemplary* nature of this punishment and this desire to free the prisoner can be precisely and surprisingly demonstrated by an internal examination of the Shroud imprint. The former can be demonstrated by the numerous wounds, inflicted in a systematic manner over almost the entire body. We can count approximately 120: this was a scourging carried out in accordance with the rules of a procedure not concerned with the number of strokes, as was the Roman custom; for the Jewish usage would not have permitted the scourgers to exceed forty strokes, lest the man being punished «be degraded».[13]

However, it would appear that the Romans were less merciful and more expert than the Jews; for they must have known how to save the man's life despite the large number of blows inflicted. In fact, the only area spared is the part of the chest in the area of the pericardium; the scourgers were sufficiently expert to know how to judge the distances, while their experience must have taught them not to strike that area, since it was the most delicate and (as we learn from modern medicine) blows inflicted there could induce death through traumatic serous paricarditis. In such an eventuality the scourgers themselves would have been personally answerable to the judge.

But these are not the only interesting details we note when examining the Shroud. The type of scourge is the *flagrum taxillatum* which fully merited the epithet *horribile* (Horace). The use of this makes it clear that the Man of the Shroud cannot have been a Roman citizen, who would had to have been beaten with rods.[14] Speaking of this question, Cicero says the rods, which were reserved for citizens, were "more honorable"!

The goads were little pointed balls of metal or animal bone and were arranged in pairs along leather thongs or cords. These goads have left marks in two clear arcs which converge on two focal points. This not only tells us the number of scourgers involved, but also reveals that this type of scourging was much more precisely geometrical than the type normally inflicted on men condemned to death on the cross. In the

[12] *Mt* 27:21; *Lk* 23:20; *Jn* 19:12.
[13] *Deut* 25:3; cf. *2 Cor* 11:24.
[14] Cf. *Acts* 22:25.

latter case, they were usually scourged naked as they trod the path to the place of execution, their arms tied to the cross-piece behind their shoulders — i.e. in a geometrically confused fashion.

But the 'language' of the Shroud becomes even more precise when we consider the areas of the left scapular and above the right scapular, which were in contact with the heavy *patibulum*. Here we find two broad imprints showing clear signs of the *flagrum:* an obvious indication that these areas were wounded before the beam was tied to the shoulders.

This 'before' and 'after' gives us a subtlety which is in full agreement with Pilate's subsequent capitulation in the face of the crowd. He feared political involvement with a « supposed king of the Jews » — Rome did not pardon such weaknesses — and so he pronounced a second sentence: « You will go to the cross ! ».

Thus the Shroud demonstrates and documents the fact that this scourged Man was not granted the liberation promised Him.

THE CROWNING WITH THORNS

The fact and manner of the crowning with thorns are expressed in precise, albeit epigrammatic style by the Gospels: « They placed a crown of thorns on his head ».[15]

Legal experts will no doubt be amazed at the infliction of this punishment which diverged from Roman penal procedure: nowhere else do we read that any other prisoner in Roman history was crowned with thorns.

The manner in which this was carried out, however, gives the lie to artists who have almost universally depicted a method of crowning quite contrary to oriental customs. In the East, kings were crowned with precious diadems placed on top of the head. Pilate can easily be exonerated from blame for the occurrence itself, for he presumably met Jesus after He had been scourged, not expecting to see Him done up as a mock king, hastily improvised by the soldiers in response to His declaration of royalty made during the trial, and received by Pilate with the

[15]   *Mt* 27:29; *Mk* 15:17; *Jn* 19:2.

sardonic smile we glimpse in the Gospel text: « So you are a king? » [16]

However, Tiberius Cæsar would have been unlikely to have protested against this infringement of penal procedure, should ill wishers have informed him ...

But the manner in which this was carried out is documented in a surprising manner by the imprint on the Shroud: the entire area of the cranium, from the occiput to the bregma, is spattered with trickles of blood, while the brown aspect of the whole area makes one think of the sweat mixed with blood which drenched the matted hair, preparing the conditions for the imprint we see today.

We must also mention the remarkable morphology of the blood, which is evidently pre-mortal bleeding, i.e. blood which clotted in accordance with the well-known physiological process and could not have been forged with a brush.

The Evangelist further notes that, after the scourging and the crowning with thorns, Jesus' clothes were put on again;[17] this is an important piece of information, as it was an exception to the rule, for the condemned men were scourged naked along the way in accordance with the Roman usage. This explains the clothes. On the Shroud we can see that the wounds inflicted previously on the shoulders by the scourgers have preserved their original form despite their having been pressed against the heavy wood. This could not have been the case if there had been no garment protecting the shoulders which had already been lacerated.

THE HELP GIVEN BY SIMON OF CYRENE

Another exception to the rule can be seen in the contribution made by Simon of Cyrene. Some may imagine this was an act of compassion on the part of the soldiers or friends accompanying the sad procession — but quite the contrary ! This was a question of false mercy to enable Him too continue as far as Calvary, which was now close at hand — that is all !

[16] *Jn* 18:37.
[17] *Mk* 15:20.

The swellings which can be noted on the face of the Man of the Shroud are clear evidence: since His hands were tied to the beam, these contusions were caused by the inevitable impacts with the ground during the falls which must have taken place. These, along with concussion of the brain, might have been too much for that tortured Man — and His executioners did not want to forgo the 'spectacle' of the king of the Jews ... on the cross ! Normally, if a man condemned to death died by accident, the punishment was considered to be at an end, and the corpse (only if requested) was given to the relatives. Otherwise wild dogs, vultures and carrion crows completed the execution, or else the body was consigned to the common grave.

THE INSCRIPTION OF THE CROSS

« Over his head they put the charge against him ».[18]

Why this further piece of information? Because the normal practice was to nail the tablet bearing the name of the condemned man together with the feet. This is archæologically demonstrated by a find made in Jerusalem in 1971. Professor Nicu Haas found the heels of John of Ezechiel (or Hezekiah) fixed side by side by a long nail to which, on the outer part, between the head of the nail and the heels, was still found clinging the remains of a small tablet of acacia wood. On this tablet the name of the crucified man was inscribed.

The imprint of the Man of the Shroud's feet, however, reveals that these were arranged with the left foot over the right. It would have been very difficult to nail the charge over His feet placed one over the other, for this was an exceptionally large charge, written in three languages: Hebrew, Greek and Latin. The tablet bore not only His name, but also the accusation for which He had been sentenced: King of the Jews. The size of the lettering, which was « read by many »,[19] suggests a plate measuring at least 60 × 20 cm. (2 ft. by 8 ins.).

[18] *Mt* 27:37.
[19] *Jn* 19:20.

THE CRUCIFIXION

While the description found in the Gospels is scanty in the amount of information divulged concerning the technique of crucifixion, examination of the Shroud presents a profusion of detail. This is because the internal evidence is supplemented by unsuspected technical elements.

When making a painstaking examination of the Shroud, we might ask whether those who carried out the sentence made any choices in the technique of execution selected. We can be quite certain that they did not opt for a method which could have reduced the pain and have lengthened the agony, in view of the fact that the Sabbath was close at hand. In fact, nails — the *atrocis crucis* (Tertullian) — were chosen in preference to ropes. What is more, these were placed in the carpi and not in the distal region, as was the case for John of Ezechiel. The thumb driven over into the palm of the hand, as seen on the Shroud, clearly shows lesion of the medium nerve.

The axonometry of the movements deduced from a study of the angles of the blood-trickles on the forearms with the latter shows an initial slumped position on the cross. This would have led inevitably to a rapid death through asphyxia or orthostatic collapse. This could only have been avoided if there were at once available the physical means to heave the body up into a raised up position. This would have permitted the crucified Man to breathe and prolong His agony for a short period. This was easily achieved by simply nailing the feet with the knees considerably bent. This is precisely what is shown by the 35° angle of the trickle of blood from the left wrist and the corresponding movement of the body to the right, shown by the direction of the blood which flowed down as far as the right elbow.

The nature of these movements and the different direction of the blood on the forearms mean we can rule out any kind of support at the perinæum which could have prevented, or at least diminished, the shooting pains from the median nerve caused, during a long agony, by continuous, forced rubbing against the nail.

Can we fit into this reconstruction of the movements the derision of the Pharisees at the foot of the cross? « You can't — you're not capable — of saving yourself ! » [20] — as if to say: « However great your

---

[20] *Mt* 27:42.

efforts, you can't manage to save yourself ! » This degree of refinement — nails and bent knees — would have been bound to have killed any crucified man in the space of only a few hours; yet this should not make Pilate's amazement surprise us, when, at sunset, he learned first from Joseph of Arimathæa and then from the centurion [21] that Jesus was dead.

His experience in this field had given him various cases, depending on the customary manners of crucifixion. Evidently the executive power, in this case, had opted for a hasty solution to the problem.

DEATH AND THE PIERCING OF THE SIDE

« ... and he bowed his head and gave up his spirit ».[22]

This detail of the bowed head can be clearly demonstrated in the case of the Man of the Shroud. It can be shown from the linear distance between the sterno-clavicular joint and the line of the mouth. This is that of a man with his head considerably bent. The Gospels say quite explicitly of Jesus that He « bowed his head and gave up his spirit ». *Rigor mortis,* which set in shortly after death, fixed the body in that position, now shown on the funerary sheet with which it was in contact in the tomb, when the head was still bowed on to the chest.

«One of the soldiers pierced his side with a spear, and at once there came out blood and water».[23]

That this too was not part of normal practice can be seen from the fact that at Jerusalem *crurifragium* was customary. The Gospels described its being employed for the thieves, and the recent archæological discovery at Jerusalem reveals that John of Ezechiel's tibias are, in fact, broken.

The piercing of the side is another unique detail in the history of crucifixions at Jerusalem. The Shroud shows striking evidence of it: in the right hemithorax, at 13 cm. from the sternum, between the fifth and sixth ribs, can be seen a wound from a sharp implement, 4 cm. (1½ ins.) wide (Roman lances at the time of Jesus are max. 1½ ins. wide). The

[21] Cf. *Mk* 15:44.
[22] *Jn* 19:30.
[23] *Jn* 19:34.

outflow of blood and water transferred on to the Shroud presents the characteristics of post-mortal blood: clots surrounded by a halo of serum, as evidenced by the different coloration.

These are some of the most important exceptions from the normal, shown by an examination of the internal evidence of the Shroud, which can be seen to be in full harmony with the Gospel account of the Passion of Christ.

PASTORAL IMPACT OF THE MESSAGE EXPRESSED BY THE SHROUD

I think an examination of the Shroud will bring us to identify the person who was wrapped in it, venerated through the centuries and preserved at Turin, with Jesus of the Gospels. For Christian believers, the basis of this « religious fact » has been summarized by Vatican II in its Christocentric vision as actualized in the sacred Liturgy, the « high point and source » of the Church's life. This life comes from the Father, in the Spirit, to « unite all things in Christ ».[24]

It is well-known that this liturgical aspect of the mystery of the passion, death and resurrection, renewed in the Eucharistic Liturgy, is connected with a liturgical prescription concerning the Altar-cloth for every celebration of the Divine Liturgy. This has been so from the very earliest days of liturgical worship. At the local council held in 325 at the Baths of Trajan in Rome, in the presence of 267 Bishops and the Emperor Constantine, Pope Silvester established that « the holy sacrifice of the Mass be celebrated on a cloth of linen consecrated by the Bishop, as if it were the clean Shroud of Christ ».[25]

Thus for 1654 years, a slight but continuous link with the Shroud via a liturgical prescription which has never been abolished has reminded the faithful of Christ in the completeness of the central and irreplaceable mystery of His passion, death and resurrection, depicted on the Shroud and renewed on all the altars of the world.

And now today, thanks to the powerful means of scientific research

[24] *Eph* 1:10.
[25] Labbé, *Scr. Conc.,* p. 1542.

and social communications, this visual 'document' can become audio-visual, if used to supplement catechesis on the Passion of Christ. It permits us not only to announce, but to demonstrate and reconstruct facts, movements and realities which bear witness to the historicity of the Jesus of the Gospels, and « to contemplate some of the authentic features of the adorable physical appearance of our Lord Jesus Christ », as Pope Paul VI of holy memory expressed in a voice tinged with emotion on the occasion of the first ever televised exposition of the Shroud.

The fact that the Shroud is an important aid to exegetical studies and to catechesis as well as an effective help towards conversion is of world-wide importance, immeasurable by the most precise statistical checks, but hidden within the invisible relationship of souls with God.

We see a model of the conversion of a repentant soul in terms of desire, longing for and also finding of the love of God in the words which flowed from the pen and heart of St. John, quoting Zechariah's prophecy at the moment of impact of the soldier's lance: « They shall look on him whom they have pierced »,[26] revealing the secret and the meaning of that source of blood and water which he saw gushing from the spear-wound made by the Roman soldier. That blood and water can be clearly seen on the right hemithorax of the Man of the Shroud.

Pastors of souls from all the continents of the earth, who have understood the validity and pastoral impact of the message of the passion, death and resurrection of Christ, presented in the light of evidence from the Shroud, have not hesitated to insert this specialized catechesis into their diocesan pastoral programmes, entrusting it to catechists who have been rigorously trained by courses of study and equipped with suitable visual and audio-visual instruments which facilitate communication, but, above all, as should be the case for persons dedicated to a genuine apostolate, who give abundant witness of an authentically Christian life.

[26] *Jn* 19:37.

BIBLIOGRAPHY

1. PAUL VI, Apostolic Exhortation *Evangelii Nuntiandi (Insegnamenti di Paolo* VI, vol. XIII, p. 1439, Typ. Pol. Vat. 1975).

2. *Dei Verbum*, 4: *AAS* 58, 1966.

3. *Dichiarazione dei Padri Sinodali*, in *L'Osservatore Romano*, 27 October 1974.

4. *Lumen Gentium*, 8: *AAS* 57, 1965.

5. *Ad Gentes*, 5: *AAS* 58, 1966.

6. PAUL VI, *Discorso ai Membri del « Consilium de laicis »* (2 October 1974): *AAS* 66 (1974) 568.

7. *Dignitatis Humanæ*, 13: *AAS* 58 (1966) 939.

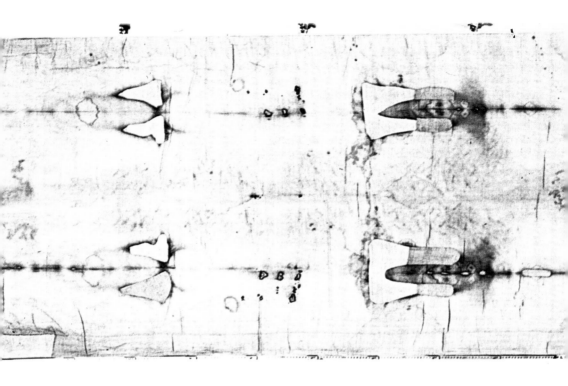

This linen funeral sheet (14' 3¾" x 3' 7½"), of herringbone weave, is perhaps the most revealing *corpus delicti* available to scholars in reconstructing the criminal action to which it testifies: judicial murder through crucifixion. It is the funeral sheet of a man who, before being put to death on the cross, was subjected to a particular kind of scourging, and to a crowning with thorns never recorded by historians in the case of other crucified men. His right hemithorax is marked by a spear wound, and he was wrapped naked in the sheet without being washed. The faintness of the imprint would suggest that this body did not undergo decomposition, which would inevitably have affected the

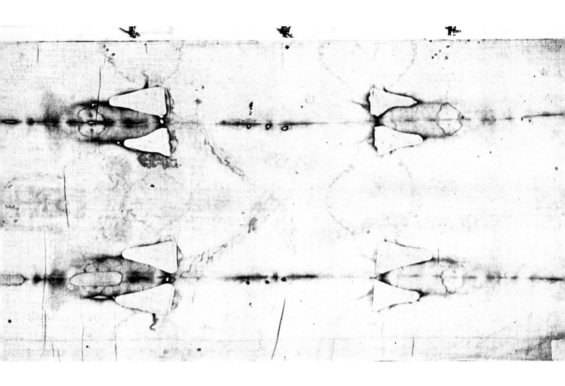

sheet's condition. The blood imprints on the Shroud are arguments against the ancient assertion that the Lord's body could have been removed by His disciples. These imprints were made from blood that flowed before death, and from blood that flowed after death; this latter blood set, whereas the former blood clotted. Experiments show that both types of blood can be transferred exactly, through the fibrinolytical action of aloes and myrrh, within a fixed period of time: about 36 hours' contact. This is the number of hours which, according to Catholic tradition, Christ lay in the sepulchre before His Resurrection.

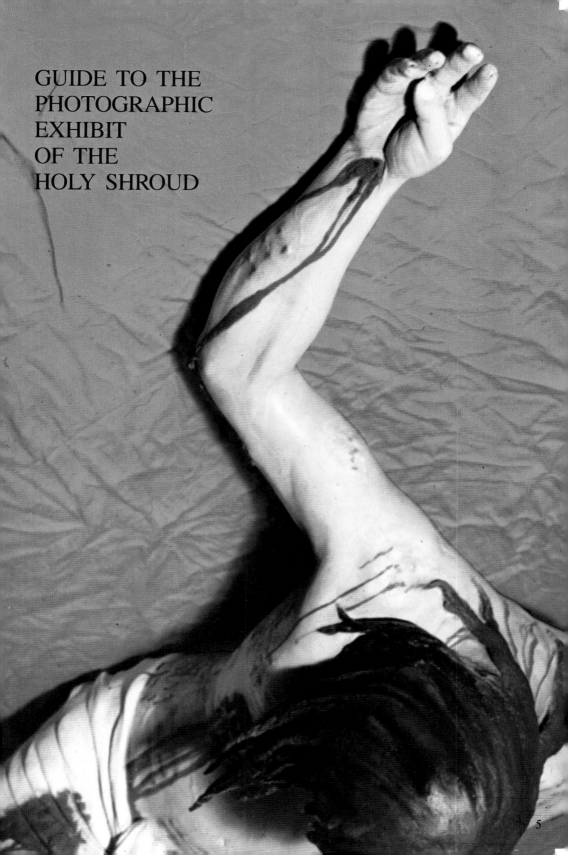

GUIDE TO THE PHOTOGRAPHIC EXHIBIT OF THE HOLY SHROUD

THE HOLY SHROUD

AN AUTHENTIC DOCUMENT
OF THE PASSION OF CHRIST

Panel n. 1

Christian tradition has always thought that the Holy Shroud was an authentic document of the Passion of Christ: science is proving that this is exact.

Panel n. 2
The twilled linen cloth of the Shroud, many times enlarged.

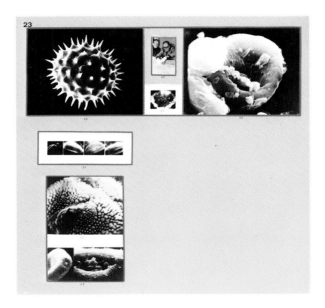

Panel n. 3
In this weave, the Swiss criminologist Max Frei has found pollen grains of plants from the area of Lake Genazareth in Palestine and pollen from plants from Turkey and from northern Europe.

He has thus traced – through pollen alone – the same map that historical documents on the Holy Shroud lead us to draw.

THIS POLLEN IS NOT THE ORIGINAL ONE ON THE SHROUD: Max Frei has published his research at the International Congress for Shroud Studies in Turin, in October 1978.

7

HISTORICAL SETTING OF THE HOLY SHROUD

Panel n. 4

Peter and John went towards the tomb. John reached the tomb first, and stooping to look in, he saw the linen cloths lying there, but he did not go in. Then Simon Peter came and went into the tomb; he saw the linen cloths lying there, and the napkin, which had been on his head, not lying with the linen cloths but rolled up in a place by itself. (Jn 20,3-7)

The primitive Church ought to have piously preserved those linen cloths, especially the Shroud as a "document" of a risen body, and not kept them away from thieves, as Mary Magdalene had already suspected. (Jn 20,2)

The twilled cloth of the Shroud enlarged many times.

There are many documents attesting the existence of the Holy Shroud through the centuries.

A fragment from the apocryphal "Gospel according to the Jews" I-II cent. that names the Shroud. In 1203-1204 Robert of Clary, who took part in the IV crusade, wrote that the Holy Shroud was shown to the public each Friday in the church of S. Mary of Blakerne in Constantinople.

Panel n. 5

Photo 8 – *The Epitaphioi.*

These "epitaphioi" or funeral shrouds, which were exposed in various Churches during the early centuries on Good Friday, show inspiration from the Holy Shroud.

Faces of Christ in art through the centuries.

From the 4th century onwards artists took inspiration from the Holy Shroud to reproduce the human likeness of Christ.

Christ Pantocrator in the painting of the apse of St. Angelo's church in Formis - Capua, Italy. (below)

Desiderio, abbot of Montecassino (1058-1087) called artists from Constantinople to paint this fresco. Note the raised eyebrow, the heavily accentuated eyes, the exaggerated cheek markings and a small triangle below the topless square on the forehead, which might be traceable to the corresponding typical blood rivulet of the Man of the Shroud.

9

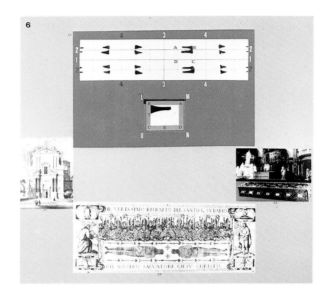

Panel n. 6-7

About 1261 the Shroud was taken to France, first to Lirey, then to Chambéry. In 1452 it was given by Margareth of Charny to Ann of Savoy and placed in a chapel of the church in Chambéry. Here the Shroud was partly burnt in a fire in 1532 and mended in 1534.

In 1578 the Holy Shroud was taken to Turin in Italy by Duke Emanuel Filibert of Savoy so that St. Charles Borromeo, Archbishop of Milan, could venerate it without crossing the Alps to Chambéry.

SCIENTIFIC STUDY
OF THE HOLY SHROUD

Panel n. 8

The photographic discovery of the Holy Shroud began in 1898 with Secondo Pia. The primitive techniques of that time offered the world the first moving image of the enshrouded body, on a photographic negative.

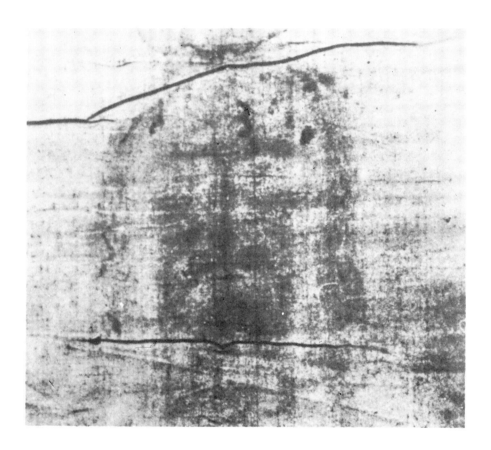

Panel n. 9
The face of Jesus: positive photograph (Pia, 1898).

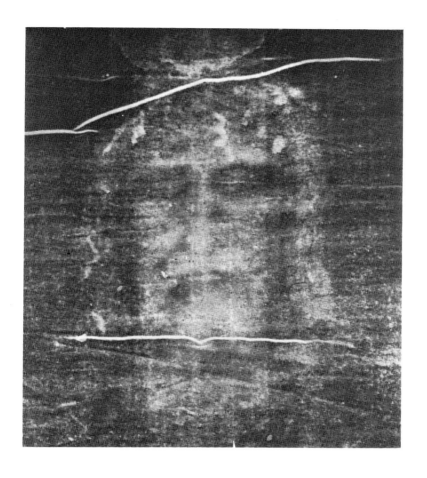

Panel n. 10
The face of Jesus: negative photograph (Pia, 1898).

Panel n. 11

Later photographs were taken by Giuseppe Enrie in 1931 which were technically perfect.

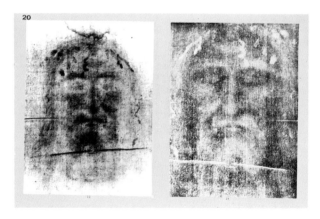

Panel n. 12

J.B. Judica Cordiglia photographed the Holy Shroud again in 1969 in color and using ultraviolet rays and Wood-light gave prominence to all organic substances: blood, saliva, sweat, aloes, myrrh, etc.

Panel n. 13

The Holy Face in a negative photograph – Wood's light (J.B. Judica Cordiglia, 1969).

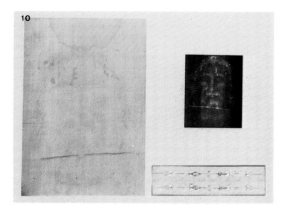

Panel n. 14
Advances in photographic techniques have gradually revealed the remarkable reality lying behind the precious linen.

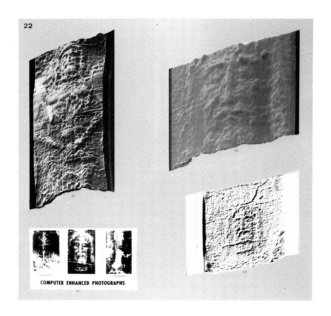

COMPUTER ENHANCED PHOTOGRAPHS

Panel n. 15
In March 1977 the First U.S.A Conference for Shroud studies was held at Albuquerque (New Mexico). Cap. J. Jackson and Eric Jumper of Colorado Springs revealed that the image on the Shroud encoded three-dimensional information: no forger could have made it.

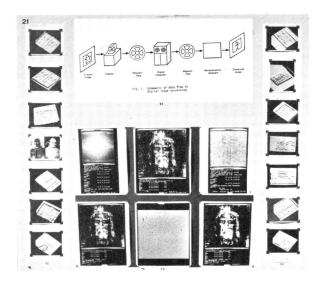

Donald Lynn and D.H. Janney of Pasadena worked on computer aided image enhancement and analysis of the Holy Shroud photographs.
a) Purified image
b) The vertical and horizontal structure of the weave of the cloth.
c) The weave of the cloth has been suppressed in image.
d) The difference between the original and the purified photograph.

Panel n. 17
Strongly contrasted enhanced version of the image produced by scanning and digitizing the ultra violet photograph by Judica Cordiglia.

Panel n. 18
The ratio of the ultraviolet images to infrared. (Lynn).

THE SCOURGING
OF THE MAN OF THE SHROUD

And as Jesus was going up to Jerusalem, he took the twelve disciples aside, and on the way he said to them: 'Behold, we are going up to Jerusalem, and the Son of Man will be delivered to the chief priests and the scribes and they will condemn him to death, and deliver him to the Gentiles to be mocked and scourged''.

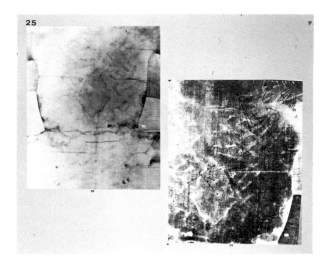

Panel n. 19

The shoulders and the loins of the Man of the Shroud.

The back of the Man of the Shroud shows clear lacero-contusions as left by the scourge, known as the "flagellum taxillatum". It was a whip the thongs of which ended in sharp little weights (taxilli) made of pointed metal or bony spheres.

J. Cordiglia 1969, Wood-light: *traces of blood trickles.*

The traces of blood trickles on the upper right shoulder and those on the central area of the back have different direction. They lead one to think that the Man of the Shroud was bent during the scourging.

Panel n. 20

High pass filtered and contrasted version of Shroud image (by D. Lynn), brings out features (of the dimensions of the filter - 31 × 31 pixels - or smaller).

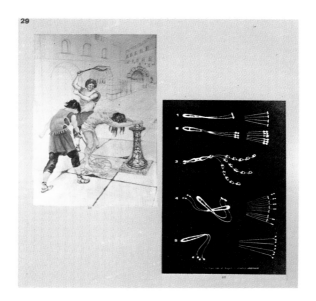

Panel n. 21

The Man was in this position.

Panel n. 22

The scourge was weighted with *taxilli* (metal or bone spheres with little spikes). - Scourges used by ancient Romans: the second was the kind used for the Man of the Shroud.

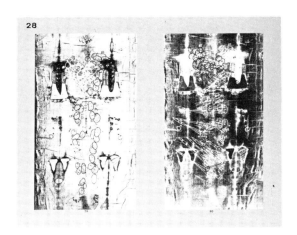

anel n. 23

1e geometrical reconstruction of the marks left by the scourging: the two converging directions e evidence that two scourgers struck the Man; the number of strokes (over 121: triple and poin-d, in pairs) reveals the *Roman method*: no fixed number. The type of scourge indicates that the an was not a Roman citizen, for whom rods would have been used. The regularity of the strokes veals he was standing still.

om a juridical point of view this fact is very important, because according to Roman law, a man ndemned to death would have been scourged along the way up to the place of execution. Thus, e Man of the Shroud was first punished for some minor offence, then crucified. The Gospels are nfirmed here again: in fact Pilate at first does not condemn Jesus to death but only to "*a les-n*", a terrible scourging. It is only in a second moment of his unjust trial that he is sentenced to ath.

anel n. 24

1e results of applying a Derivative Filter in a direction 45° clockwise from horizontal. Features .g. *strokes of the scourge*) that are normal to the direction of the gradient are displayed (D. ynn).

anel n. 25

he back of the Man of the Shroud.

anel n. 26

he "*roses*" of blood that formed along the spine reveal the curved position of Jesus during the ourging.

Panel n. 27

Lacerated contusions made by the *taxilli* the scourge on the tibias (Detail).

Panel n. 28

The right shoulder and upper part of the back, with double rivulets of blood that reveal two distinct positions of the body during, and immediately after the scourging, when he lifted himself up.

22

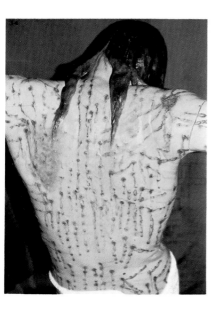

Panel n. 29
A view of the back marked by the terrible scourging.
(Reconstruction by G. Ricci).

Panel n. 30
The scourging of Jesus: reconstruction from the evidence revealed by the Holy Shroud (G. Ricci).

23

THE CROWNING WITH THORNS

Panel n. 31

"And the soldiers put on his head a crown which they have woven out of thorns, and dressed him in a scarlet cloak." (Jn. 19:12).
Msgr. Giulio Ricci: reconstruction according to the Holy Shroud.

Panel n. 32

The top of the head of the Man of the Shroud is marked by many traces of rivulets of blood caused by a crown of thorns.

Panel n. 33

"From that moment Pilate sought to release him, but the Jews cried out: 'If you release this ma you are not Caesar's friend; everyone who makes himself a king sets himself against Caesar." (19,12).

"Pilate said to them: 'Shall I crucify your king?' The chief priests answered: 'We have no ki but Caesar' Then he handed him over to them to be crucified". (Jn 19,15b-16).

28

FROM THE PRAETORIUM
TO THE CALVARY

Panel n. 34
Jesus willingly accepts the cross.

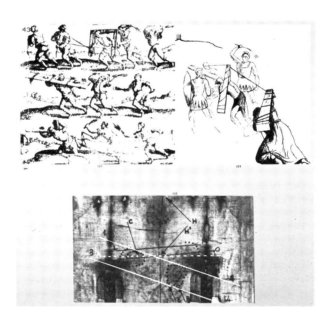

Panel n. 35
The parallel lines show the crosswise direction of the beam tied to the outstretched arms of the Man of the Shroud; two marks can be seen – one in the left scapular area, and one in the right above-scapular region – left by the crossbeam or *patibulum*.

Panel n. 36
Archaeological evidence and literary text document that prisoners only carried the horizontal beam... the vertical pole being already set up at the place of execution (See detail in fig. 34).

Panel n. 37
Crucifixion began in Asia Minor as early as the V cen. B.C., and was taken by the Romans from the Carthaginians during the Punic wars, and used especially for slaves and non citizens.

Panel n. 38
When more than one was to be crucified, they were tied together.

Panel n. 39
Oblique traces of blood on the left tibia, following the direction of a rope attached to the lower end of the beam. (Ultraviolet and Wood's light).

One can see clearly, on the imprint of the Holy Shroud, the left kneecap bruised, lacerated (4 m.) and swollen, from the falls along the way.

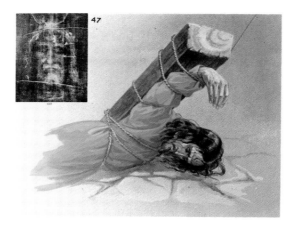

Panel n. 42

G. Ricci: reconstruction of Jesus falling for the first time.

Panel n. 43

The Holy Face shows clear evidence of bruising above the left eyebrow and in the area of the left cheekbone.

Panel n. 44

The Gospel says that His Mother, the blessed Virgin Mary, was under the cross on Calvary. In this reconstruction is imagined a possible maternal gesture if they met along the sorrowful way.

Panel n. 45
Jesus falls for the second time (Reconstruction by G. Ricci).

Panel n. 46
The centre of the forehead with clear evidence of bruising: a severe contusion, that could cause concussion.

Panel n. 47
Jesus falls for the third time. (G. Ricci - Reconstruction).

Panel n. 48
On the Holy face, the broken nasal cartilage and the large contusion round the eyesocket and on the right cheekbone are evident.

Panel n. 49
Volumetric, plastic, reproduction of the face - left and right sides - as can be reconstructed from the Holy Shroud.

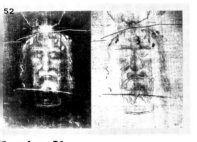

Panel n. 50
The axonometric studies carried out on the face impressed on the Holy Shroud.

Panel n. 51
The clinical condition of this Man explains very well why the cross was taken from him and handed to Simon of Cyrene to carry: *"They seized one Simon of Cyrene, who was coming in from the country, and laid on him the cross, to carry it behind Jesus"*. (Lk 23, 26). This too is an absolute exception to Roman law.

Panel n. 52
"And there followed him a great multitude of people, and of women who bewailed and lamented him". (Lk 23, 27).

Panel n. 53

Tradition says that one of these women, named Veronica, wiped the Holy Face with a linen cloth. Evidence from the Holy Shroud does confirm that his face was wiped in some moment between the Pretorium and Calvary, because of the different directions of the blood rivulets on the back of his head and on his face.

Panel n. 54

The soldiers *"took his garments and made four parts"*. (Jn 19,23). The blood on the left forearm, parallel to that of the wound on the wrist, was probably caused by the stripping off of his garments, which reopened the previous wounds of the scourging.

Panel n. 55

Crucifixion was very much practiced in antiquity and could be carried out in various ways, for example, with ropes or nails. Crucifixion with nails was *"the most atrocious"* Tertullian II cen. A.D.

For the Man of the Shroud, like Jesus, nails were used: clearly visible are the holes made by the nails in the wrists of the Man.

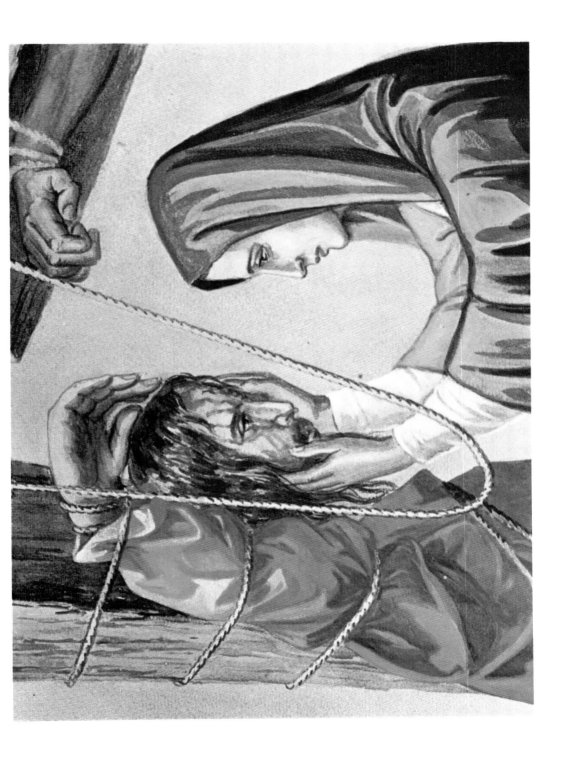

38

THE CRUCIFIXION

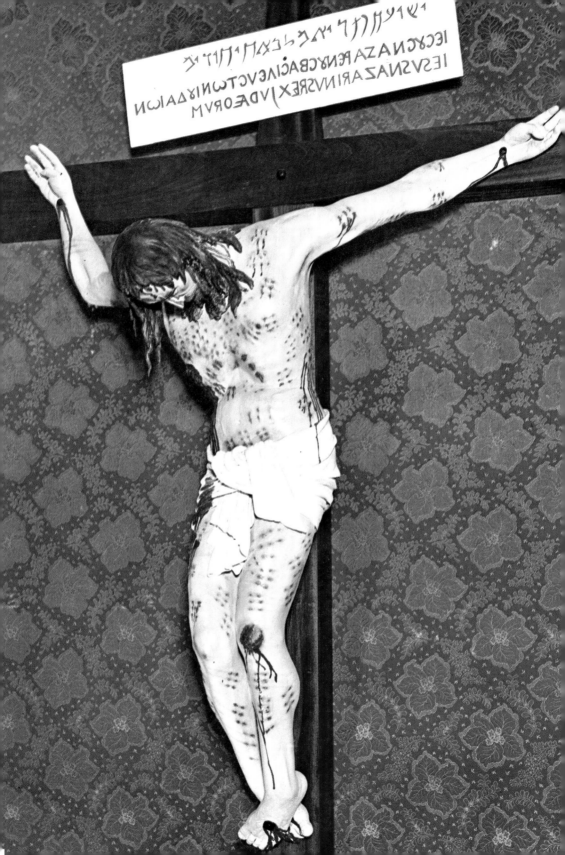

There they crucified him, and with him two others, one on each side and Jesus between them."
n 19,18).

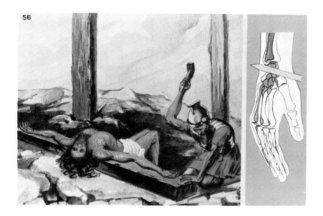

Panel n. 57
Crucifixion. (Reconstruction by Msgr. G. Ricci).

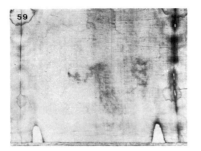

Panel n. 58
Most evident is the hole of the nail in the right fo

Panel n. 59
Study of the angles that reveal the two main movements of Jesus on the cross, in the first part of his terrible agony (left arm).

Panel n. 60
The hole of the nail and the *"rose"* blood on the top of the right foot*: th confirms that the left foot was naile over the right one.

lood running in two directions from the wound of the nail in the left wrist at an angle of 35°, akes it possible to reconstruct the first stages of the agony on the cross with the initial sagging f the body and the subsequent effort of an upwards movement, to avoid asphyxiation.

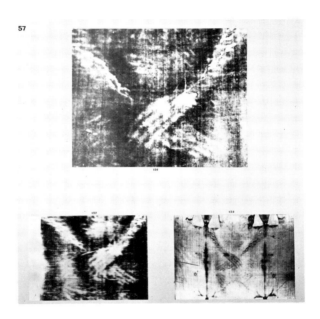

Panel n. 62

The nails located in the wrists have produced the characteristic imprint found on the Holy Shroud: the thumb is bent in towards the palm of the hand and is not visible; this was caused because the nail damaged the median nerve - a motor nerve which has a reflex action on the thumb, but also a sensory nerve which, when wounded, causes excruciating pains. (Note also the metacarpal crown with its lacerated contusions caused by contact with the rough surface of the beam).

Panel n. 63

Sketch of the movements of Jesus on the cross, during the first part of his three-hour agony; la he remained fixed in the raised-up position, by muscular cramps due to anoxemia, and conseque lactic acid.

Panel n. 64

The outstretched arms of Jesus on the cross: a loving *"bridge"* for all mankind toward Our Heavenly Father.

Panel n. 65

G. Ricci: Crucifix according to the Holy Shroud.

Panel n. 66

"He bowed his head and gave up his spirit". (Jn. 19:30).

Panel n. 67

G. Ricci: Detail from the first sindonic Crucifix (Assisi - Pont. Regional Seminary).

Panel n. 68

st century Roman lances, discovered in Roman soldiers' tomb in Jerusalem: the maximum width f the blade is 1.6 inches, like the wound in the side of the Man of the Shroud.

45

Panel n. 69

The wound in the right side of the Man of the Shroud.

At the top of the wound a 4 cm opening can be seen made by a spear and this corresponds to the maximum cutting edge of a Roman spear. Such a spear was found in a Roman soldier's tomb of the first century.

Colour photograph of the right side.

In the colour photograph the wound is visible, so too is the outflow of blood which clotted on contact with the air and was surrounded by the dried serous liquid.

... the blood and the water mentioned by St. John (Jn 19,34).

Painting of the Sacred Heart.

The image of the Sacred Heart and the relative providential devotion takes origin from the unfathomable suffering and love which had the better expression through the type of death Jesus chose to endure.

"Behold the heart that so much loved men, and so little love receives in return!" (Jesus to S. Mary Margaret Alacoque)

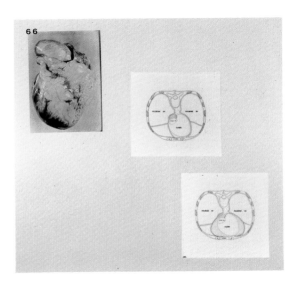

Panel n. 70

A fissured heart as a result of miocardic infarction and consequent death by haemopericardium.

Panel n. 71

The Man of the Shroud died in a raised up position, after having bowed his head. Modern cardiologists explain that he most probably died from infarction, because only in this case can we find *"blood and water"* (serum and crassamentum) in the pericardic sac, already sedimented. Opening the chest and pericardic sac of such a person we would find two distinct components of the human blood: serum, and the crassamentum.

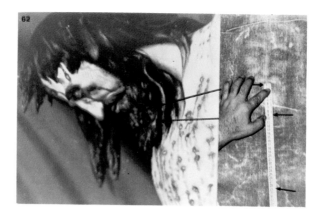

Panel n. 72

The head of the Man of the Shroud bowed even in death.

After deducting 7.2 inches from the thorax, there only remain 3.6 inches from the mouth to the sternum-clavicular joint; the winding of the Shroud under the chin reduces the linear distance to 2.8 inches: in other words, the head of the Man is resting forward on the breast.

AND HE WAS BURIED…

Panel n. 73

"After this, Joseph of Arimathea came and took away his body" (Jn 19,38).

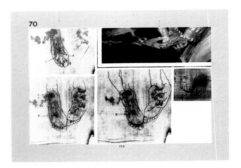

Panel n. 74

The left heel of the Man of the Shroud, with marks left by three fingers of the hand of one of his bearers.

Panel n. 75

"They took the body of Jesus and bound it in linen cloths with the spices... There was a new tomb where no one had ever been laid. So they laid Jesus there". (Jn 19,40). The body of Jesus was left unwashed because of the lack of time, in view of the closeness of the Sabbath (day of absolute rest): he was wrapped temporarily, lengthwise, in the long expensive shroud bought by Joseph of Arimathea. These exceptional circumstances, and the maternal love and care with which a woman (note the psychology of the gestures) – very probably his Mother – deliberately wrapped the body, paying particular attention to the face and to the most significant wounds, have made it possible for us to have an imprint of the front and back of the whole body that had remained naked after the soldiers had divided his garments.

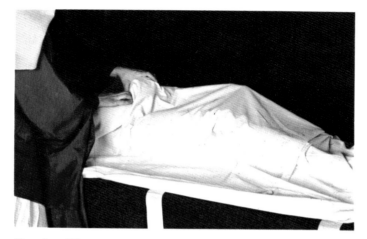

Panel n. 76

The sheet was tucked under the left hand so as to reach the wound of the nail on the right wrist.

Panel n. 77

The blood trickle on the right arm, with its "8" shape near the wrist, partly duplicated by osmosis, proves the gesture in Fig. 76.

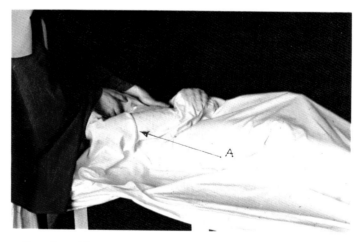

Panel n. 78

Further testimony to the maternal, deliberate wrapping of the body: inside the arms the sheet was tucked in, so as to reach the wound on the right side of the chest. Without this gesture, we would not have the moving evidence of the love of Jesus: the open wound in his side and signs of his heart, split open by miocardic infarction, before the soldier opened his chest three hours after he had died.

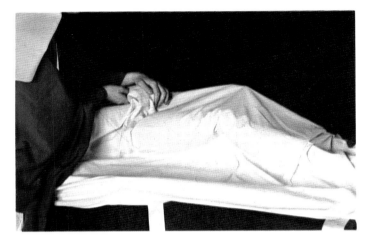

Panel n. 79
The tucking in round the forearms has caused a lengthening and distorting of the imprint of the arms in respect to the correct anatomical position.

Panel n. 80
Wrapping the right femur.

Panel n. 81
The imprint of the thighbone is very clear in the imprint of the front part of the Man of the Shroud's body, but it is missing in the dorsal imprint: his Mother had tucked the top part of the sheet round the limb and the lower part of the sheet after - the latter therefore did not have direct contact with the body and has no imprint.

53

Panel n. 82

The sheet was very long so it was pleated at the lower third of the tibias: this is why the frontal imprint of the legs is interrupted, whilst the back imprint of the tibias is complete.

Panel n. 83

The sheet was also tucked in under the fingers of the crossed hands.

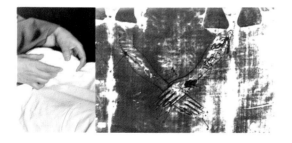

Panel n. 84

We see - especially in the ultraviolet photographs - the imprint of the finger tips protruding beyond the anatomical line of the hands, because the sheet had been tucked in under the crossed hands.

the ultraviolet photograph, with Wood's light, one can even see pleats made in the sheet over e tibias.

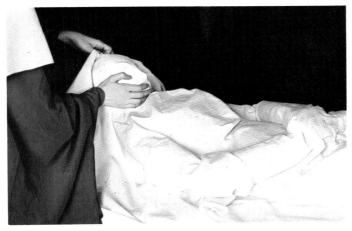

Panel n. 86
The sheet was wrapped over the face and on the head, where it formed a large fold.

anel n. 87
ver the head, the doubled cloth, not being in direct contact with the body, has received no im-rint: betweeen the front and back imprints of the head, there are 5.6 inches called the *"epicranic ace"*.

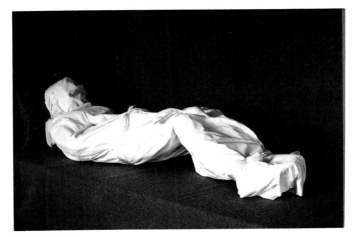

Panel n. 88
He lay like this for about thirty-six hours...
Experiments done recently by Prof. Baima Bollone of Turin and Prof. Rodante of Siracuse (Italy) have proved that this is the ideal time for obtaining with aloes and myrrh and humidity, an imprint of the same kind as the one on the Shroud.

Panel n. 89

G. Ricci, *reconstruction: the Resurrection.*

Jesus took up his glorified life: free of physical laws and unseen by anyone, passed through the white-veined red rock of that most glorious tomb in history. With the simplicity of the works of God, the Holy Shroud and the napkin (sudarium) were left on the ledge in the tomb to testify to the fact that his glorious body had been removed by divine intervention and not by thieves.

Panel n. 90

G. Ricci, reconstruction: Jesus condemned to death.

THE FINGERS POINTED AGAINST HIM ARE UNDOUBTEDLY THOSE OF ALL HUMAN-TY WHO, THROUGH THE MYSTERIOUS ACTION OF SIN WHICH AFFECTS EACH PE-SON, ACCUSE HIM, THE INNOCENT ONE; THEY POINTED AT HIM AS DEPOSI MOCK KING, DERIDED, REJECTED AND CONDEMNED. YET JESUS OFFERS US SALV TION IN HIS BLOOD AND WILL CALL US "BLESSED" IF WE BELIEVE IN GOD AN LOVE ONE ANOTHER.

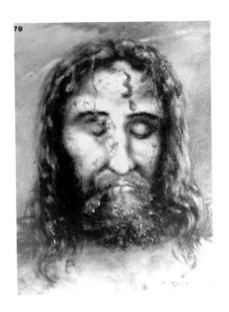

Panel n. 91
G. Ricci: Painting of the Holy Face,
from the Holy Shroud.

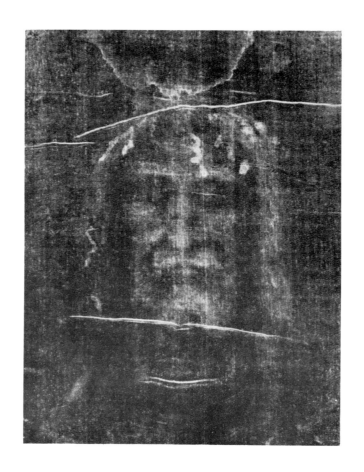

Panel n. 92
The Holy Face (Enrie 1931).
BUT WE SEE JESUS, WHO FOR A LITTLE WHILE WAS MA-
DE LOWER THAN ANGELS, CROWNED WITH GLORY AND
HONOUR BECAUSE OF THE SUFFERING OF DEATH, SO
THAT BY THE GRACE OF GOD HE MIGHT TASTE DEATH
FOR EVERY ONE. FOR IT WAS FITTING THAT HE, FOR
WHOM AND IN WHOM ALL EXISTS BRINGING MANY SONS
TO GLORY, SHOULD MAKE THE PIONEER OF THEIR SAL-
VATION PERFECT THROUGH SUFFERING. (Heb 2,9-10)

STATISTICAL APPENDIX

A brief period of catechesis on the Passion with documentation from the Shroud using some photographic exhibitions — only eleven staged, lasting an average of two months — presents the following data:

visitors: 539,288

average per day: 6,064

signature only: 18,786

signature with comments: 15,818

Quantitative analysis of the comments

— Praise and blessings to the Lord;
— gratitude for the redemption;
— repentance and accusation of own responsibility for the passion and death of Christ;
— intention to lead a Christian life and real conversions: altogether 90%.
— For the remaining 10% the comments range from encouragement to polemic and include infrequent declarations of unbelief.

I think we can conclude that, to the eyes of the man of today, the Holy Shroud appears, especially to those far from the faith and from Christian practice, with the authenticity of its message: «See my hands, my feet and my side: IT IS I! », offering to all the possibility of an experience of a personal encounter with «Him Whom we have pierced».